Young Learner's

Number

Writing Book

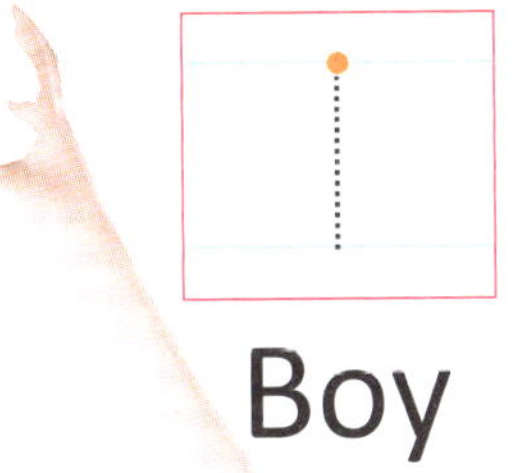

Boy

Dice

Candles

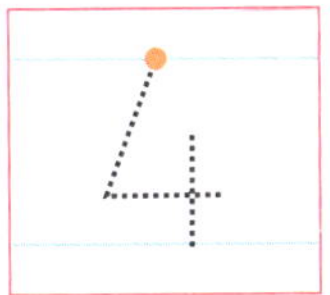

Doughnuts

Trace and Learn: 1

Date: ____________ Grade: ____________ Teacher's Signature: ______________

Practice Time!

Use red colour to circle number I.

1			1			5	1	2		1		1
2			7			4				8		7
6	4	1	9			1				1	8	1
1			1	0	1	2	1	4	1	3		2

Date: ____________ Grade: ____________ Teacher's Signature: ______________

Trace and Learn: 2

2	2	2	2	2	2	2	2	2
2	2	2	2	2	2	2	2	2
2	2	2	2	2	2	2	2	2
2	2	2	2	2	2	2	2	2
2	2	2	2	2	2	2	2	2
2	2	2	2	2	2	2	2	2
2	2	2	2	2	2	2	2	2

Date: ____________ Grade: ___________ Teacher's Signature: ______________

Practice Time!

Two pictures are same. Circle them.

Date: ____________ Grade: ___________ Teacher's Signature: ______________

Trace and Learn: 3

Date: ____________ Grade: ___________ Teacher's Signature: ____________

Practice Time!

Colour any three bugs with red colour and the remaining with blue colour.

Date: ____________ Grade: ____________ Teacher's Signature: ______________

Trace and Learn: 4

4	4	4	4	4	4	4	4	4
4	4	4	4	4	4	4	4	4
4	4	4	4	4	4	4	4	4
4	4	4	4	4	4	4	4	4
4	4	4	4	4	4	4	4	4
4	4	4	4	4	4	4	4	4
4	4	4	4	4	4	4	4	4

Date: ____________ Grade: ____________ Teacher's Signature: ____________

Practice Time!

Circle number '4'.

2	6	3	9	4	2	8	3	4	5	2
7	4	8	0	8	6	4	0	6	9	4
3	2	5	4	2	2	0	5	4	2	0
4	8	6	7	7	6	4	3	7	3	9
7	9	3	4	8	3	8	4	8	7	4
4	5	9	2	5	4	2	9	6	2	2

Date: ____________ Grade: ____________ Teacher's Signature: ____________

Date: ____________ Grade: ____________ Teacher's Signature: ______________

Practice Time!

Count the number of petals in each flower and write it in the box.

Date: ____________ Grade: ____________ Teacher's Signature: ______________

Date: ____________ Grade: ____________ Teacher's Signature: ____________

Practice Time!

Count the objects and draw a line to the correct number.

6

5

3

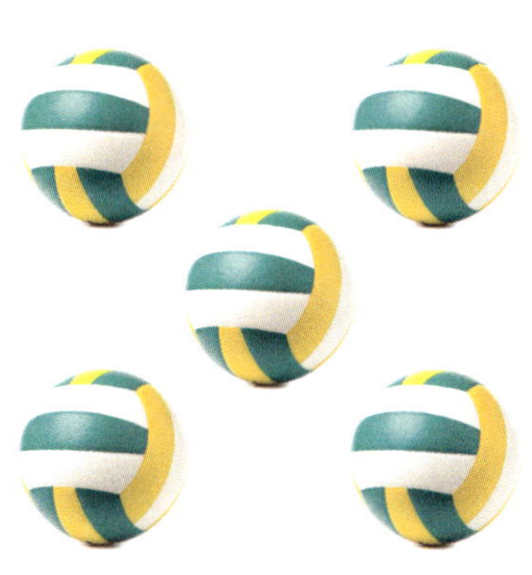

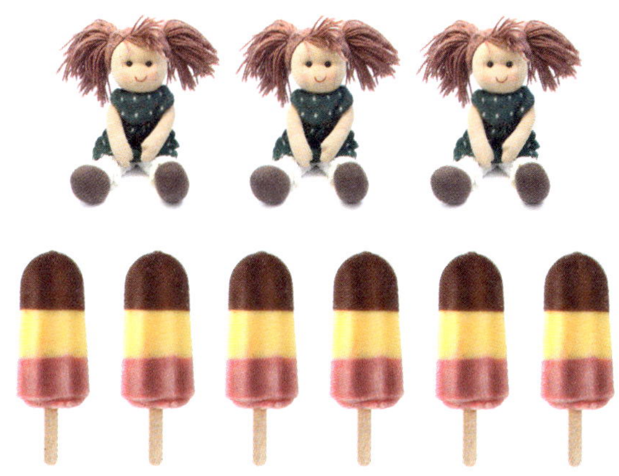

Date: ___________ Grade: ___________ Teacher's Signature: ___________

Trace and Learn: 7

Date: ____________ Grade: ___________ Teacher's Signature: ____________

Practice Time!

Colour any seven balls.

Date: ___________ Grade: ___________ Teacher's Signature: ___________

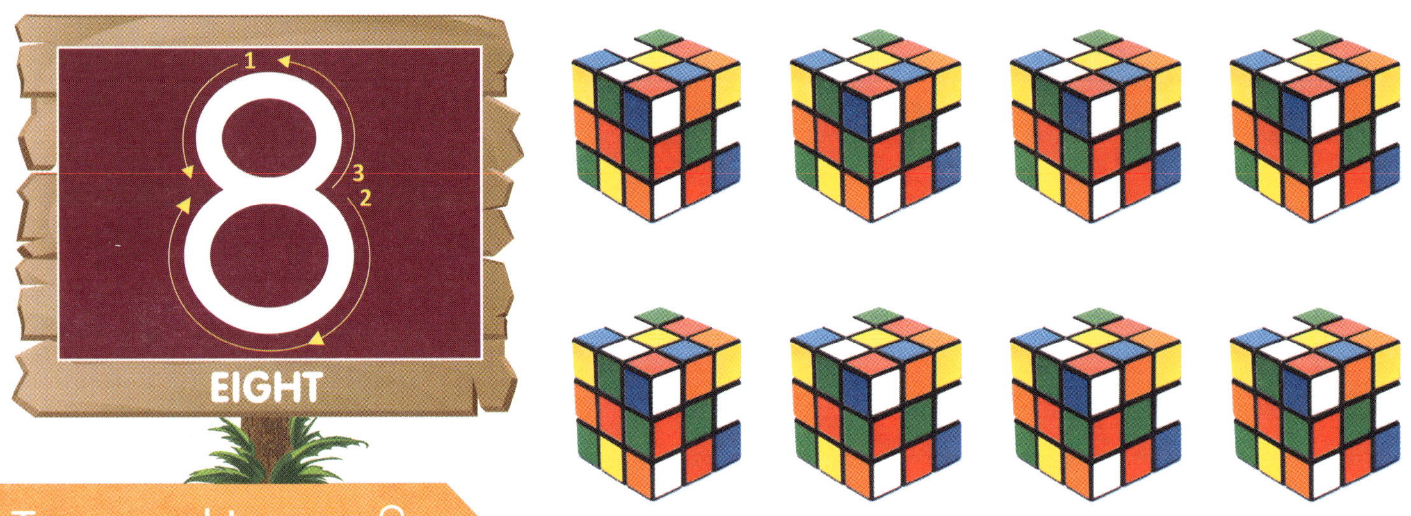

Trace and Learn: 8

8	8	8	8	8	8	8	8	8
8	8	8	8	8	8	8	8	8
8	8	8	8	8	8	8	8	8
8	8	8	8	8	8	8	8	8
8	8	8	8	8	8	8	8	8
8	8	8	8	8	8	8	8	8
8	8	8	8	8	8	8	8	8

Date: ___________ Grade: __________ Teacher's Signature: ____________

Practice Time!

What comes after?

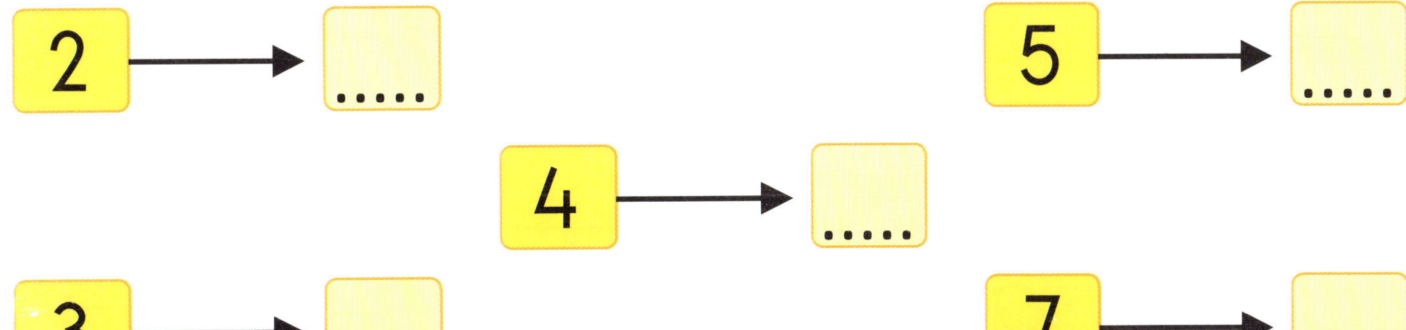

Date: ____________ Grade: ____________ Teacher's Signature: ____________

Date: ____________ Grade: ___________ Teacher's Signature: ______________

Practice Time!

What comes before?

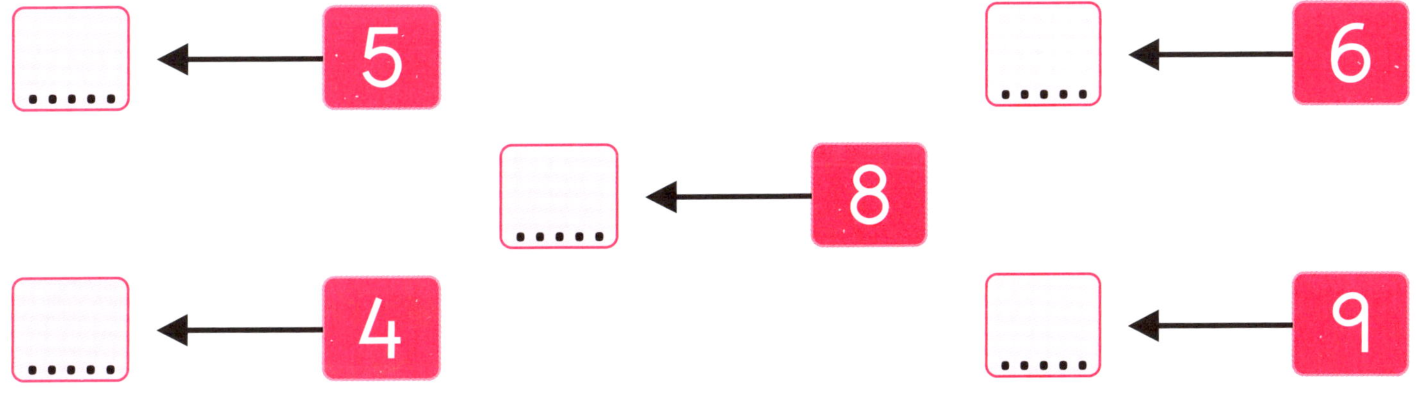

Date: ____________ Grade: ____________ Teacher's Signature: ____________

Trace and Learn: 10

10	10	10	10	10	10	10	10	10
10	10	10	10	10	10	10	10	10
10	10	10	10	10	10	10	10	10
10	10	10	10	10	10	10	10	10
10	10	10	10	10	10	10	10	10
10	10	10	10	10	10	10	10	10
10	10	10	10	10	10	10	10	10

Date: ____________ Grade: ____________ Teacher's Signature: ____________

Practice Time!

Count and circle the correct number.

7 10 6

Date: ____________ Grade: ___________ Teacher's Signature: _____________

Complete the counting from 1 to 10.

Date: ___________ Grade: __________ Teacher's Signature: ____________

Activity Time 2

Count and write the number of objects in the given box.

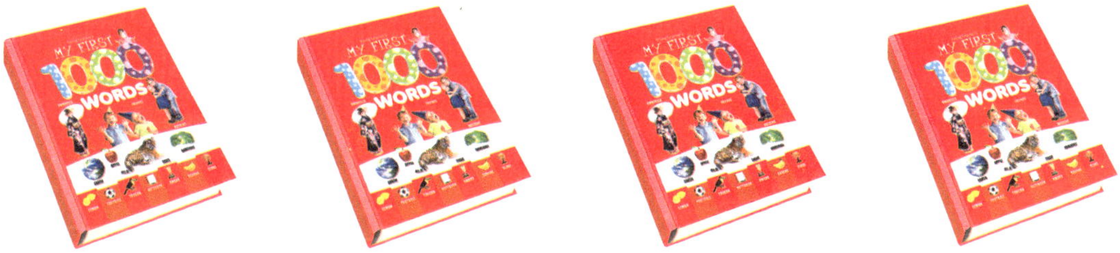

Date: ____________ Grade: ___________ Teacher's Signature: _____________

Activity Time 3

Count the objects in each box and draw a line to the correct number.

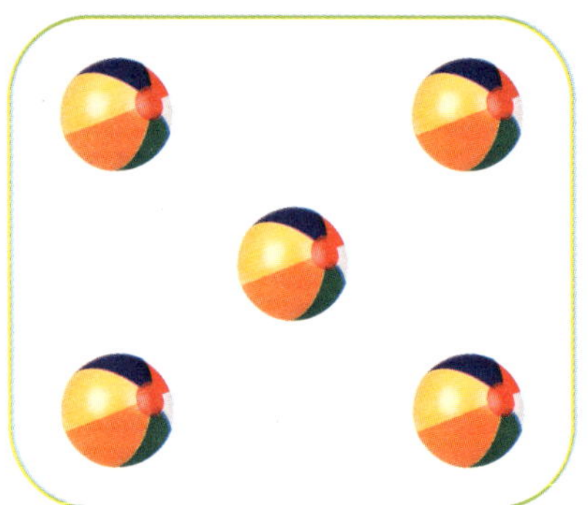

6

10

8

9

4

1

3

5

Date: ___________ Grade: __________ Teacher's Signature: ____________